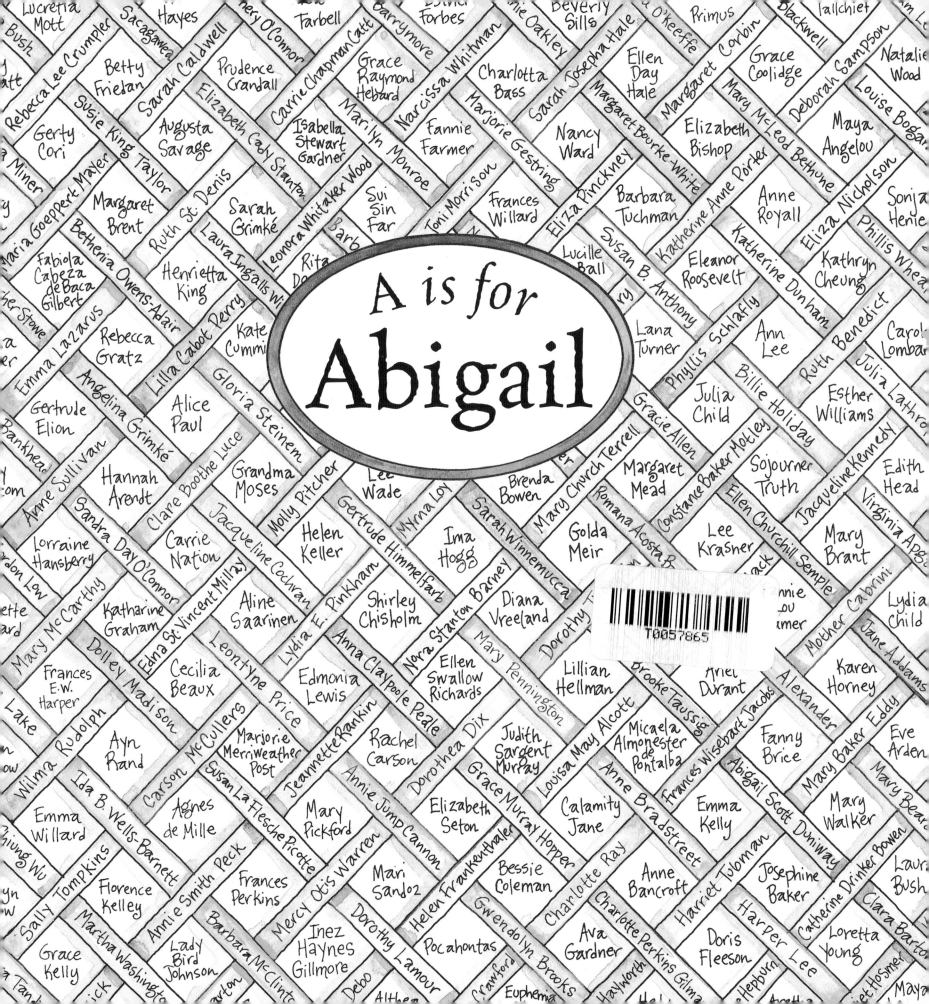

A is for Abigail

A is for Abigail

An Almanac of Amazing American Women

by LYNNE CHENEY

Illustrated by

ROBIN PREISS GLASSER

A Paula Wiseman Book
Simon & Schuster Books for Young Readers
New York   London   Toronto   Sydney   New Delhi

In memory of my mother and grandmothers —L. C.

For all the fathers who encouraged their daughters—but mostly for mine —R. P. G.

ACKNOWLEDGMENTS

I'd like to thank the supremely talented Robin Preiss Glasser, whose illustrations have time and again touched my heart. I'd also like to acknowledge my research assistant Elisabeth Irwin, who, with intelligence and enthusiasm, helped us straighten out the most challenging historical tangles; Jacqueline Preiss Weitzman, who helped Robin and who demonstrated once again her discerning eye for the details that make history come alive; and Faith Hamlin, who is Robin's literary agent and her friend.

My gratitude to Kristina Peterson for launching this project and to Rick Richter for seeing it to completion. For this book as well as for *America: A Patriotic Primer,* Brenda Bowen and Lee Wade proved to be the best editor and designer that an author and illustrator could ever hope to have, and I want to thank them as well as Hilary Goodman, Dorothy Gribbin, and Lisa Ford. The entire team at Simon and Schuster has been superb.

I also want to acknowledge the American Enterprise Institute and, in particular, one of my colleagues there, Jeane Kirkpatrick, a trailblazer for women, whose knowledge, insight, and clarity of expression are an inspiration for all. I am also grateful to AEI President Chris DeMuth for his fine leadership and for his support of scholars who take on all manner of projects—even children's books.

My special thanks to Robert Barnett, lawyer extraordinaire, who has, with great good cheer, donated many an hour to *A is for Abigail* as well as to *America: A Patriotic Primer.* —L. C.

SIMON & SCHUSTER BOOKS FOR YOUNG READERS • An imprint of Simon & Schuster Children's Publishing Division • 1230 Avenue of the Americas, New York, New York 10020 • Text copyright © 2003 by Lynne V. Cheney • Illustrations copyright © 2003 by Robin Preiss Glasser • All rights reserved, including the right of reproduction in whole or in part in any form. • SIMON & SCHUSTER BOOKS FOR YOUNG READERS is a trademark of Simon & Schuster, Inc. • For information about special discounts for bulk purchases, please contact Simon & Schuster Special Sales at 1-866-506-1949 or business@simonandschuster.com. • The Simon & Schuster Speakers Bureau can bring authors to your live event. For more information or to book an event, contact the Simon & Schuster Speakers Bureau at 1-866-248-3049 or visit our website at www.simonspeakers.com. • Also available in a Simon & Schuster Books for Young Readers hardcover edition • Book design by Lee Wade • The text for this book was set in Celestia Antique. • The illustrations for this book were rendered in black ink, watercolor washes, and colored pencil. • Manufactured in China • 0522 SCP • First Simon & Schuster Books for Young Readers paperback edition September 2016 • 10 9 8 7 6 5 4 3 2 • The Library of Congress has cataloged the hardcover edition as follows: • Cheney, Lynne V. • A is for Abigail: an almanac of amazing American women / Lynne Cheney ; illustrated by Robin Preiss Glasser.—1st ed. • p. cm. • Summary: Each letter of the alphabet is represented by an important woman in the history of the United States, as well as others in her same field of accomplishment. • ISBN 978-0-689-85819-2 (hardcover) • ISBN 978-1-4814-7959-2 (pbk) • ISBN 978-1-4424-2408-1 (eBook) • 1. Women—United States—Biography—Juvenile literature. 2. United States—Biography—Juvenile literature. 3. Alphabet books—Juvenile literature. [1. Women—Biography. 2. United States—History. 3. Alphabet.] I. Preiss-Glasser, Robin. II. Title. • CT3207.C48 2003 • 973'.09'9—dc21 • 2003007381

The quotation by Mary Lyon in the notes for the E page appears courtesy of Mount Holyoke College, Archives and Special Collections.

Editor's Note: Archaic spelling, capitalization, and punctuation in historical quotations have been modernized throughout the text.

"I look for the day... when the only criterion of excellence or position shall be the ability and character of the individual; and this time will come." -Susan B. Anthony

In Abigail Adams's time, women could not go to college, become professionals, own property once they were married, or vote. The transformation of women's lives from then to now is one of our great national narratives, an inspiring story that our children deserve to know. I especially hope this book will help them learn about the women who brought about the transformation, whether it's Abigail Adams telling John to "remember the ladies" and seeing to her own daughter's education, Mary McLeod Bethune starting a school for African-American girls, or Elizabeth Cady Stanton and Susan B. Anthony devoting their lives to securing the vote.

There is also another story to tell, and that's of the amazing things women have achieved, often before their rights and capabilities were fully recognized. I think of Abigail Adams, who, without legal or political sway, managed to support her family financially by running the Adams farm; of Harriet Tubman, born enslaved, freeing herself and hundreds of others from slavery; of Rosalyn Yalow, ignoring stereotypes about women's scientific abilities and doing the work that would win a Nobel Prize.

Often there were encouraging parents behind these women achievers. William Mitchell set his daughter Maria on the path to becoming a famed astronomer by teaching her to study the stars. Novelist Zora Neale Hurston's mother, Lucy, urged her children to have high aspirations by telling them to jump at the sun.

Reaching high and working hard are recurring themes in the lives of those in this book, and so, too, are being brave, never giving up, and caring deeply about the welfare of others. America's amazing women have much to teach our children—and much inspiration to offer us, as well.

Lynne Cheney

A is for ABIGAIL ADAMS, who knew that women should be heard.

in the new Code of Laws which I suppose it will be necessary for you to make I desire you would Remember the Ladies

While he[r] husband, John[,] was helping t[o] create the America[n] nation, ABIGAIL ADAMS ran the family farm and took car[e] of their four children. John woul[d] become our second president. Joh[n] Quincy, John and Abigail's oldest son, woul[d] become our sixth president[.]

As the Revolutionary War approached, Abigail's treasured pewter spoons were melted to make bullets.

Abigail decided whom to hire, what to plant, and when to harvest, and she prided herself on her skill. "The barley looks charmingly," she wrote to John in the spring of 1776.

1776, WHEN JOHN WAS CONSIDERING WHAT THE LAWS FOR THE NEW NATION SHOULD BE, SHE WROTE TO HIM, "I DESIRE YOU WOULD

In Abigail's time, most people didn't think it was important for girls to be educated—but Abigail knew better and said so.

Much of their fifty-four-year marriage was spent apart as John was helping to create the new country. Abigail wrote him hundreds of letters.

Although her house was small, Abigail willingly gave shelter to soldiers fighting for America's cause.

Abigail wove homespun cloth during the Revolutionary War and made clothes for the whole family.

When John was able to come home, Abigail was very happy. She called him her "dearest friend."

1764 — 1784

ABIGAIL AND JOHN ADAMS LIVED IN THIS HOUSE IN BRAINTREE, MASSACHUSETTS.

B is for ELIZABETH BLACKWELL
and others who wanted to heal.

In 1849 ELIZABETH BLACKWELL became the first woman to earn a medical degree. She encouraged others who wanted to prevent illness and help the sick.

"I do not wish to give [women] a first place, still less a second one—but the most complete freedom to take their true place, whatever it may be."

Dr. L. Rosa Minoka-Hill

Dr. Mary Walker

Dr. Rebecca Lee Crumpler

Mary Ann Bickerdyke

Sally Tompkins

Dr. ELIZABETH BLACKWELL FIRST WOMAN DOCTOR

Dr. Emily Blackwell

Dorothea Dix

Lillian Wald

Dr. Virginia Apgar

Born in slavery, Susie King Taylor nursed wounded soldiers during the Civil War. In 1902 she described her experiences in a memoir.

Called "the Angel of the Battlefield" for her work during the Civil War, Clara Barton helped found the American Red Cross in 1881.

In 1947 Dr. Gerty Cori and her husband won the Nobel Prize in medicine. She was the first American woman to do so.

Dr. Virginia Apgar devised the Apgar Score, a test that has been used since the 1950s to evaluate the health of newborn babies.

ELINORE PRUITT STEWART, who homesteaded in Wyoming, wrote letters that described her hardworking life. In one she told of cooking at night so that she could cut hay during the day.

ANNIE OAKLEY, who began traveling with "Buffalo Bill" Cody's Wild West Show in 1885, demonstrated such skill with a rifle that she came to be known as "Little Sure Shot."

C is for EVELYN CAMERON and the women who went west.

EVELYN CAMERON, born in England, moved to Montana with her husband in 1889. In the decades that followed, she broke colts, pitched hay, cut down trees, fed chickens, and also created a valuable historical record by photographing the people, landscapes, and wildlife of the American West.

Cowgirl advice: "Always saddle your own horse."

In 1899 ANGIE DEBO traveled to Oklahoma with her family in a covered wagon. When she grew up, she became a historian and often wrote about the unjust way in which American Indians had been treated.

D is for EMILY DICKINSON, our country's greatest poet.

Although she seldom left her home in Amherst, Massachusetts, EMILY DICKINSON explored the world through her imagination.

There is no Frigate like a Book
To take us Lands away—
Nor any Coursers like a Page
Of prancing Poetry—
This Traverse may the poorest take
Without oppress of Toll—
How frugal is the Chariot
That bears the Human soul.

The daughter of former slaves, MARY McLEOD BETHUNE knew that education was the key to opportunity. A school she founded for African-American girls later became Bethune-Cookman College.

"Education is the great American adventure, the world's most colossal democratic experiment."~ Mary McLeod Bethune

E is for the EDUCATORS, the women who taught us well.

Knowing that girls should have a good education, EMMA WILLARD founded Troy Female Seminary in 1821.

MARÍA CADILLA DE MARTÍNEZ was a leader in teaching and preserving Hispanic and Puerto Rican culture.

MARY LYON, who founded Mount Holyoke College, opened the doors of higher education to women.

ANNE SULLIVAN helped Helen Keller, who could not see or hear, to learn.

ANNE CARROLL MOORE showed that libraries could be joyful places for children.

Martha Washington

Abigail Adams

Dolley Madison

Sarah Polk

F

Margaret Taylor

Abigail Fillmore

F is for the FIRST LADIES, who have graced our nation from the start.

Lucretia Garfield

Frances Cleveland

Caroline Harrison

Ida McKinley

Edith Roosevelt

Helen Taft

Eleanor Roosevelt

Bess Truman

Mamie Eisenhower

Jacqueline Kennedy

Lady Bird Johnson

Pat Nixon

Elizabeth Monroe

Louisa Adams

Anna Harrison

Letitia Tyler

Julia Tyler

Jane Pierce

Eliza Johnson

Lucy Hayes

Mary Todd Lincoln

Julia Grant

Ellen Wilson

Grace Coolidge

Edith Wilson

Florence Harding

Lou Hoover

Rosalynn Carter

Nancy Reagan

Barbara Bush

Hillary Rodham Clinton

Betty Ford

"Somewhere out in this audience may even be someone who will one day follow in my footsteps and preside over the White House as the president's spouse. I wish him well!"
—Barbara Bush at Wellesley College commencement, 1990

Laura Bush

Frank Leslie's Illustrated Newspaper

No. 1.—Vol. 1.   "ALL THE NEWS ABOUT WOMEN IN THE NEWS"   PRICE, TEN CENTS.

G is for
MARY KATHERINE GODDARD
and others who brought us news.

NELLIE BLY *exposed injustices and traveled far to get good stories. On her most famous trip, which started in 1889, she broke the globe-circling record of Phineas Fogg, the fictional hero of* Around the World in Eighty Days.

IDA B. WELLS-BARNETT *denounced violence against African Americans in the* Memphis Free Speech, *a newspaper she co-owned. In 1892 mobs destroyed the newspaper's offices.*

In 1775 MARY KATHERINE GODDARD became the publisher of the *Maryland Journal*. In 1777 she was commissioned by the Continental Congress to print the first signed copies of the Declaration of Independence so that they could be sent to the states.

MARGARET BOURKE-WHITE *worked for* Life *magazine, a publication designed for photojournalists. Many of her photographs of the Great Depression and World War II and after are classics today.*

SARAH JOSEPHA HALE *became the exacting editor of* Godey's Lady's Book, *an influential magazine, in 1837.*

IDA TARBELL's *articles about the Standard Oil Company, written from 1902 through 1904, set a new standard for investigative journalism.*

Until she died in 2001, KATHARINE GRAHAM *headed a media empire that includes the Washington Post newspaper and Newsweek magazine. She loved what she did and felt that it mattered. "How could anything," she asked, "be more fun?"*

In the late nineteenth and early twentieth centuries, journalist SUI SIN FAR *took up the cause of Chinese Americans. Her work was published in both newspapers and magazines.*

Popular advice columnist ANN LANDERS *had a snappy way of putting things. "The naked truth," she wrote, "is always better than a best-dressed lie."*

DALE MESSICK's *comic strip starring intrepid reporter Brenda Starr was the first to be syndicated by a woman.*

H is for ANNE HUTCHINSON, who defended her beliefs.

In 1634 Puritans William and ANNE HUTCHINSON and their eleven children sailed from England to the Massachusetts Bay Colony, seeking a place where they could worship as they chose. Anne's beliefs were different from those of the colony's leaders, however, and when she set forth her views and gained enthusiastic followers, the Massachusetts General Court put her on trial. She defended herself with bravery and eloquence, but was banished from the colony forever.

I is for LAURA INGALLS and other girls of America's past.

YOU DON'T HAVE TO BE A GROWN-UP TO BE PART OF HISTORY.

When LAURA INGALLS was a child, her family, like many, looked for land they could farm for a living. From 1869 to 1879 she moved with her family from the woods to the prairie, to Walnut Grove, Minnesota, to De Smet, South Dakota. When she grew up, she wrote books about the many places she had lived.

In 1852 seven-year-old FANNIE PECK, usually barefoot, walked the Mormon Trail alongside her family's wagon.

In 1777, when sixteen-year-old SYBIL LUDINGTON learned that the British were burning Danbury, Connecticut, she sounded an alarm to rally patriot forces.

In 1855 teenager ANN MARIA WEEMS disguised herself as a boy and escaped from slavery.

J is for ANNA JARVIS, who loved her mother very much.

Because of ANNA JARVIS, Mother's Day became a national holiday in 1914.

Sonora Dodd, inspired by Mother's Day, thought of Father's Day. She was raised by her father.

In 1942 movie star Hedy Lamarr co-patented a concept that is today important for cell phone and satellite communication.

Martha Coston developed a system of signal flares used during the Civil War.

Inspired by West African mothers, Ann Moore invented a baby carrier.

Bette Nesmith Gra[...] invented a correcti[...] fluid for typists and parlayed it int[...] a multimillion-dollar busines[...]

In 1924 Gertrude Muller started a company to market the potty seat she had invented.

K is for MARY KIES and other inventors and entrepreneurs.

In 1809 MARY KIES received the first U.S. patent granted to a woman. Her invention, a method of weaving straw and silk together, advanced the art of hat making.

In the 1950s MARION DONOVAN invented the first disposable diaper.

The daughter of immigrants, ESTÉE LAUDER started a cosmetics company in 1946 that is a multibillion-dollar business today.

ROSE MICHTOM, an immigrant from Russia, created the first teddy bear in 190[...]

Stephanie Kwolek invented Kevlar, the ultrastrong fiber used in everything from bulletproof vests to spacecraft.

Margaret Rudkin started the Pepperidge Farm bakeries in 1937.

In 1938 Katherine Blodget[...] received a patent for "invisible" glass, an inventi[...] that makes everything from telescopes to eyeglasses easier to see through.

Olive Ann Beech and her husband Walter started Beech Aircraft in 1932. Their first Beechcraft was the Staggerwing.

Fannie Farmer decided to measure precisely the ingredients in her recipes. Her cookbook, first published in 1896, has sold some 4 million copies.

MADAME C. J. WALKER *developed hair-care products for African Americans. The company she started in 1906 was a great success.*

Selling everything "from hat to hem," **HATTIE CARNEGIE,** *who immigrated to America as a child in 1892, built a multimillion-dollar fashion empire.*

In 1888 Elizabeth Boit cofounded a company to manufacture ladies' underwear.

In 1886 Josephine Garis Cochran invented the first practical dishwasher.

In the 1870s **MARGARET KNIGHT** *invented the machine-made paper bag.*

1903 Alabama native Mary Anderson invented a windshield wiper.

Ellen Louise Demorest made a fortune marketing dress patterns in the nineteenth century.

In business with her father, Kate Gleason marketed machinery that made beveled gears for early twentieth-century automobiles.

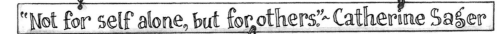

MOTHER CABRINI, an Italian nun who became an American citizen in 1909, helped found orphanages, schools, and more than seventy hospitals.

Before World War II, HENRIETTA SZOLD brought thousands of Jewish boys and girls out of Hitler's Germany.

GRACE ABBOTT worked to help those who were new to America. In 1908 she became head of the Immigrants' Protective League.

L is for
JULIA LATHROP
and those
who have
lifted
others up.

As the first head of the Children's Bureau, a government agency created in 1912, JULIA LATHROP worked to make the lives of babies and children safer and better.

After escaping from slavery, HARRIET TUBMAN risked her life and freedom by returning to the South more than a dozen times to help others who were enslaved escape.

In 1889 JANE ADDAMS established Hull House, a place in Chicago where she lived among people in need and found ways to help them.

In 1932 AMELIA EARHART became the first woman to fly solo across the Atlantic Ocean.

In 1983 DR. SALLY RIDE became the first American woman in space.

"The eye that directs a needle in the delicate meshes of embroidery will equally well bisect a star with the spiderweb of the micrometer." ~ Maria Mitchell

DR. ELLEN OCHOA became the first Hispanic woman astronaut in 1990.

DR. MAE JEMISON became the first African-American woman in space in 1992.

M is for MARIA MITCHELL
and all who look to the skies.

In 1953 JACQUELINE COCHRAN became the first woman to break the sound barrier.

In 1921 BESSIE COLEMAN became the first African-American woman to be licensed as a pilot.

Before she retired in 1940, ANNIE JUMP CANNON classified some 350,000 stars.

In 1847 MARIA MITCHELL discovered a comet in the night skies. By the 1860s her reputation as an astronomer was so exalted that Vassar College built this observatory for her.

MARIA MONTOYA MARTINEZ

HARRIET HOSMER

HELEN FRANKENTHALER

ALMA THOMAS

N is for LOUISE NEVELSON
and other creators of
beautiful things.

*"To be surrounded by beautiful things has
much influence upon the human creature;
to make beautiful things has more."*
—Charlotte Perkins Gilman

MARY CASSATT

LOUISE NEVELSON

GEORGIA O'KEEFFE

SARAH PEALE

"I stand before you to proclaim tonight: America is the land where dreams can come true for all of us." ~ Geraldine Ferraro, in her acceptance speech for the 1984 Vice Presidential nomination

NELLIE TAYLOE ROSS
First Woman Governor

FRANCES PERKINS
First Woman Cabinet Member

WILMA MANKILLER
*First Woman Chief of
the Cherokee Nation*

SANDRA DAY O'CONNOR
*First Woman
Supreme Court Justice*

ESTHER MORRIS
*First Woman
Judicial Officer*

JEANNETTE RANKIN
*First Woman
Member of Congress*

O is for SANDRA DAY O'CONNOR
and others who were first.

the PERFORMERS.

Lena Horne

Aretha Frank[l]

Angela Lansbury

Ella Fitzgeral[d]

Rita Moreno

Chita Rivera

Ethel Barrymore

Kate Smith

Judy Garland

Tina Turner

Helen Hayes

Ethel Merman

Pearl Bailey

Leontyne Price

Sarah Caldwell

P is for th

Mary Martin

Fanny Brice

Mary Tyler Moore

Imogene Coca

Carol Burnett

Gilda Radner

Lucille Ball

Suzanne Farrell

Lu
Ser

Maria Tallchief

Judith Jamison

Martha Graham

Isado
Dunca

"Just don't give up trying to do what you really want to do. Where there is

love and inspiration, I don't think you can go wrong."—Ella Fitzgerald

"THE QUILT PATTERN WAS GLORIOUSLY DRAWN IN OAK LEAVES, DONE IN INDIGO; AND SOON . . .

YOUNG AND OLD WERE PASSING BUSY FINGERS OVER IT AND CONVERSATION WENT ON BRISKLY . . .

[E]ACH VIED WITH THE OTHERS IN THE DELICACY OF THE QUILTING SHE COULD PUT UPON IT, FOR

THE QUILTING ALSO WAS A FINE ART." — HARRIET BEECHER STOWE, *THE MINISTER'S WOOING*, 1859

Q is for the
QUILT MAKERS, who
brought art to everyday life.

World War II women of the military: WACs, WAVES, and WASP

R is for ROSIE THE RIVETER and women who went to war.

When American men went to fight in World War II, women filled their jobs. They worked in offices and factories, became welders and truck drivers, and made Rosie the Riveter, with her can-do attitude, a fitting national symbol. Women also served bravely in the U.S. Army, Navy, Marine Corps, Coast Guard, and Army Air Forces.

Proud of their work in building this C-47, many of the women signed the plane.

S IS FOR THE SIXTIES AND SEVENTIES AND THE SECOND WAVE

T is for TRAILBLAZERS,
the women who showed us the way.

Mary Beard insisted that women be included in history.

"I will not follow where the path may lead, but I will go where there is no path, and I will leave a trail."
—Muriel Strode

Annie Dodge Wauneka led health campaigns on behalf of the Navajo people.

Julia Morgan, renowned architect, paved the way for other women in her profession.

Marjory Stoneman Douglas alerted people to the importance of restoring the Everglades.

Amelia Bloomer advocated a freer style of dress for women.

Antoinette Blackwell helped open the ministry to women.

Charlotte Ray broke through a barrier for African-American women when she was admitted to the District of Columbia bar.

Elizabeth Peabody began the American Kindergarten movement.

Joan Ganz Cooney and Peggy Charren made television something children could like and learn from.

1800s: INDUSTRIAL REVOLUTION: Factories hire women and children.

1837

Oberlin becomes 1st coeducational college in U.S.

1838: Angelina Grimké: first woman to address a U.S. legislative body

1848

Women gather in Seneca Falls, New York; demand equality.

1843: Wagon trains begin to leave every spring for Oregon.

1851: Myrtilla Miner opens school for African-American girls in Washington, D.C.

1850s: Bloomers are introduced.

U is for US and our grand history.

1814: Dolley Madison saves precious items when British burn White House.

Sacagawea travels with Lewis and Clark through the American West.

WAR OF 1812

1805-1806

1861-1865: THE CIVIL WAR

Julia Ward Howe writes "The Battle Hymn of the Republic."

1787: Constitution signed

1861

Harriet Tubman leads raid freeing slaves.

1863

1908: Model T launched

Jovita Idar founds La Liga Femenil ... 1911

Mercy Otis Warren publishes history of Revolution. 1805

1776: The Declaration of Independence

Poetry of Phillis Wheatley, who came to Boston as a slave, published. 1770

The Daughters of Liberty make homespun clothes to protest the British.

1769

1865: 13th Amendment abolishes slavery.

1865

1903

1900: Margaret Abbott: 1st American woman to win Olympic gold medal

Mary Harris "Mother" Jones protests child labor; leads a march of mill children.

1775-1783: THE REVOLUTIONARY WAR frees America from British rule.

Anne Bradstreet's Poetry published

1650

Colonial women spin wool, weave cloth, and make soap and candles.

Wyoming Territory grants voting rights to women.

1869

Katharine Lee Bates writes "America the Beautiful."

1893

Molly Pitcher: legendary heroine of the Revolutionary War

Pocahontas saves John Smith's life.

1587

1620

Susan B. Anthony votes in New York; is arrested and fined.

1872

1879: Susette La Flesche speaks out for Indian rights.

Virginia Dare born on Roanoke Island

1607

30 of the Pilgrims on the Mayflower are female.

1876: telephone patented

Electric Light 1879

1881: Clara Barton, the "Angel of the Battlefield," founds the American Red Cross.

Juliette Gordon w organizes irl Scouts of America.

1917–1918: U.S. in WORLD WAR I

1972: Title IX insures equal access to higher education.

Barbara Walters interviews world leaders.

Sherry Lansing runs major motion picture studio.

·1913· 5,000 women march down Pennsylvania Avenue demanding to vote. VOTES FOR WOMEN

1920: 19th Amendment ratified. Women can vote.

119 women enter corps of Cadets at West Point. ☆1976☆ ·1977·

Mary Wells Lawrence's company launches "I ♥ NY" campaign.

Maya Lin selected to design Vietnam Veterans Memorial. ·1981·

1912

1921: Margaret orman is 1st iss America.

1919: Mary Pickford helps start movie company.

·1920·

MS.

First issue of "Ms. Magazine"

·1972·

WOMEN'S LIBERATION

1981: Sandra Day O'Connor appointed to the Supreme Court. Says, "Abigail Adams would be pleased."

Dr. Mary Pennington helps develop refrigeration.

Amelia Earhart crosses Atlantic. ·1928·

The miniskirt comes to America. 1965

"Sesame Street," brainchild of Joan Ganz Cooney, airs. ·1969·

1968: Diahann Carroll Stars as "Julia."

·1981·

Sally Ride: 1st American Woman in Space ·1983·

1985: Gloria Estefan brings Latin music to the world.

Dorothea Lange documents hardships.

GREAT DEPRESSION of the 1930s

·1930s·

·1964·

1964: Civil Rights Act prohibits employment discrimination.

·1986·

"The Oprah Winfrey Show" goes national.

1941–1945: U.S. in WORLD WAR II

Women rally around the war effort.

1943: Agnes de Mille choreographs musical "Oklahoma!"

Eleanor Roosevelt chairs President's Commission on the Status of Women ·1961·

1959: Barbie doll introduced.

Antonia Novello becomes Surgeon General of the US. ·1990·

1991: End of COLD WAR

Margaret hase Smith ected to U.S. enate ·1948·

·1959·

1999: Carly Fiorina becomes CEO of Hewlett-Packard.

oodle kirts

1954: Brown v. Board of Education: school segregation unconstitutional

Rosa Parks ·1955·

Lorraine Hansberry's "Raisin in the Sun" opens on Broadway.

·1990·

·2003·

tigh heels get higher.

·1951· Lucille Ball stars in "I Love Lucy." ·1953·

Susan Butcher wins Iditarod for 4th time.

·1996· Atlanta U.S. Women win 19 Gold Medals in Summer Olympics.

14 women are members of the U.S. Senate.

Jacqueline Cochran breaks the sound barrier.

The Baby Boom!

Rosa Parks refuses to give up her seat; galvanizes the Civil Rights Movement.

PEARL S. BUCK

ZORA NEALE HURSTON

SARAH ORNE JEWETT

LOUISA MAY ALCOTT

TONI MORRISON

HARRIET BEECHER STOWE portrayed the evils of slavery in her 1851–1852 novel, *Uncle Tom's Cabin.*

WILLA CATHER depicted life on the American frontier in novels like her 1918 work, *My Ántonia.*

W
is for
EDITH
WHARTON
and women writers all.

In 1921 EDITH WHARTON became the first woman to win the Pulitzer Prize in fiction. Even as a little girl she had been enchanted by language: "There was in me a secret retreat," she wrote in her autobiography. "Words and cadences haunted it like song-birds in a magic wood."

Woman's Rights Convention, 1848   "...all men and women are created equal."   Declaration of Sentiments

VOTES for Women   VOTES for Women

ELIZABETH CADY STANTON and SUSAN B. ANTHONY often worked at Mrs. Stanton's house while her children rollicked around them.

X is for the mark on the ballot.

Elizabeth Cady Stanton and Susan B. Anthony, who worked fifty years for the vote, did not live to see women's right to the ballot recognized in the Constitution. They made it possible for others to enjoy their inalienable rights.

Sojourner Truth

Lucretia Mott

Martha Coffin Wright

Lucy Stone

Susan B. Anthony

Elizabeth Cady Stanton

Carrie Chapman Catt

1920 BALLOT BOX

"There is not one foot of advance ground upon which women stand today that has not been obtained through the hard-fought battles of other women." ~ Susan B. Anthony, 1897

Y is for ROSALYN YALOW and women in science and math.

Rear Admiral GRACE MURRAY HOPPER was a pioneer in computer science.

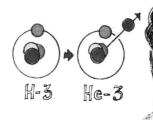

A medical physicist, DR. ROSALYN YALOW won a Nobel Prize in 1977.

H-3 → He-3

For groundbreaking work in physics, DR. CHIEN-SHIUNG WU received the National Medal of Science in 1975.

In 1983 DR. BARBARA McCLINTOCK was the recipient of the Nobel Prize for her work in genetics.

In 1943 EUPHEMIA LOFTON HAYNES became the first African-American woman to receive a Ph.D. in mathematics.

MARIA GOEPPERT MAYER won a Nobel Prize in 1963 for work on modeling the nucleus of the atom.

$$a^2 + b^2 \approx c^2$$
$$\sqrt{2}$$
$$\pi \approx \frac{C}{2r}$$

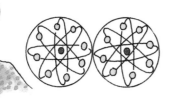

Chemist GERTRUDE ELION won the Nobel Prize in 1988 for medicines she developed.

Z is for BABE DIDRIKSON ZAHARIAS and all the women who would be strong.

Three-time World Figure Skating Champion PEGGY FLEMING won an Olympic gold medal in 1968.

MARJORIE DICKEY, 1930s softball star

In 1957 ALTHEA GIBSON became the first African American to win a Wimbledon championship.

MIA HAMM, twenty-first-century soccer star

In 1993 JULIE KRONE became the first woman to win a Triple Crown horse race.

In 1911 ANNIE SMITH PECK planted a "Votes for Women" flag at the summit of Mount Coropuna, a mountain in Peru that she was the first to climb.

At the 1932 Olympics, BABE DIDRIKSON ZAHARIAS won medals in high jump, javelin throw, and hurdles. A baseball, basketball, and golf champion as well, she was named Woman Athlete of the Year six times.

In 1926 GERTRUDE EDERLE became the first woman to swim the English Channel.

MARY LOU RETTON, in 1984, became the first American to win Olympic gold in women's gymnastics.

"I am strong. I am invincible. I am woman!" —Helen Reddy

NANCY LOPEZ was inducted into the World Golf Hall of Fame in 1989.

In 1988 and 1992 JACKIE JOYNER-KERSEE won gold medals in the seven-event Olympic competition known as the heptathlon.

In 1960 WILMA RUDOLPH became the first American woman to win three gold medals in a single Olympiad.

Notes on the Text

Hoping that this book will inspire many conversations among children and their parents and teachers, I include these notes to provide additional information. Those who wish to go further and learn more will find an abundance of material in libraries and on the Internet. A particularly important source for information about women in American history is the four-volume biographical dictionary Notable American Women, *which was published in 1971 and 1980 under the auspices of Radcliffe College.*

With about a dozen exceptions, the women in this book were born before 1950.

—L. C.

EPIGRAPH

Abigail's sentiments were offered to Winslow Warren, the son of her friend Mercy Warren, on May 19, 1780. In those days some of her wishes would not have been thought suitable for girls, but today they are apt for all of our children, daughters as well as sons.

A

Abigail wrote about the importance of virtue, honor, truth, and integrity in a letter to her son John Quincy in June 1778.

Abigail saw to it that her daughter Nabby studied Latin. On April 18, 1776, John wrote to Nabby that she should keep her Latin study a secret since it was "scarcely reputable" for a young lady to study such a subject.

The part of Braintree in which John and Abigail lived became part of the town of Quincy. Thus the Adams National Historical Park, where the house shown is located, is in Quincy, Massachusetts, today.

B

Dr. Mary Walker (1832–1919) tended to both civilians and soldiers during the Civil War. She was awarded the Congressional Medal of Honor.

For more than forty years Dr. L. Rosa Minoka-Hill (1876–1952), born a Mohawk, provided medical services to members of the Oneida tribe in Wisconsin.

Dr. Rebecca Lee Crumpler (c. 1833–1895), the first African-American woman to earn a medical degree, focused on helping women and children.

In Richmond, Virginia, Sally Tompkins (1833–1916) operated a hospital that helped sick and wounded Confederate soldiers to recover.

Dorothea Dix (1802–1887) was an effective advocate for humane treatment of the mentally ill.

When Lillian Wald (1867–1940) established the Henry Street Visiting Nurses Service to provide medical care for those who might otherwise go without it, she founded a new profession: public health nursing.

Emily Blackwell (1826–1910) followed her older sister, Elizabeth, in becoming a doctor. She helped her sister found the New York Infirmary for Women and Children.

Mary Ann Bickerdyke (1817–1901) ministered to sick and wounded Union soldiers during the Civil War. The men she helped called her "Mother Bickerdyke."

C

Evelyn Cameron (1868–1928) took a photograph of herself standing on top of her horse in 1912. She called it "Self-Portrait Standing on Jim."

The cowgirl advice comes from Texan Connie Reeves, who is 101 years old.

D

Edna St. Vincent Millay (1892–1950) started writing poetry as a girl, became famous when she was twenty, and won the Pulitzer Prize when she was thirty-one.

Rita Dove (1952–), who was the youngest person and the first African American to become poet laureate of the United States, won the Pulitzer Prize for *Thomas and Beulah*, a volume of poems about her grandparents.

Dorothy Parker (1893–1967), noted for her humor, observed that "wit has truth in it."

In addition to writing poetry, Sylvia Plath (1932–1963) wrote an autobiographical novel, *The Bell Jar*.

Besides being a poet, Maya Angelou (1928–) is the author of autobiographies, most notably, *I Know Why the Caged Bird Sings*.

Marianne Moore (1887–1972) said that poetry should present "imaginary gardens with real toads in them."

Adelaide Crapsey (1878–1914) created a demanding five-line poetic form known as the cinquain.

Frances E. W. Harper (1825–1911) reached a wide audience with antislavery poems and her novel, *Iola Leroy*.

Muriel Rukeyser (1913–1980) often used her poetry to protest violence and injustice.

Phillis Wheatley (c. 1753–1784), who came to America as a slave, began writing poems when she was thirteen.

Anne Bradstreet (1612–1672), who came to New England with the Puritans, authored the first collection of verse written in America.

Beginning in 1950 with a Pulitzer Prize for *Annie Allen*, Gwendolyn Brooks (1917–2000) won many awards for her poetry.

Using traditional forms, Leonie Adams (1899–1988) created powerful lyric poems.

Poet Harriet Monroe (1860–1936) founded an influential magazine called *Poetry*.

In addition to volumes of poetry, such as *Nets to Catch the Wind*, Elinor Wylie (1885–1928) wrote historical novels.

Of the many poems Katharine Lee Bates (1859–1929) wrote, the most famous is "America the Beautiful," which she composed in Colorado.

Hilda Doolittle (1886–1961), also known as H. D., enriched her poetry with her knowledge of the classical world.

In a poem about women who write poetry, Amy Lowell (1874–1925) wondered "what it is that makes us do it."

Anna Hempstead Branch (1875–1937) once described the joy of looking at the world as children do, so that even "common things seem shapèd of the sun."

Lucy Larcom (1824–1893) often published her verse in magazines for children such as *St. Nicholas* and *Youth's Companion*.

Pulitzer Prize winner Louise Glück (1943–) once wrote that she loved poems "that seemed so small on the page but that swelled in the mind."

A California poet, Ina Coolbrith (1841–1928) published *Songs from the Golden Gate* in 1895.

Eunice Tietjens (1884–1944) was a poet, a war correspondent, and the author of books for children and young people, including *The Jaw-Breaker's Alphabet of Prehistoric Animals*, which she wrote with her daughter.

Louise Bogan (1897–1970) thought poetry should express the hard-won insights of personal experience.

During the Harlem Renaissance, Anne Spencer (1882–1975) published poems in which images illuminated many topics, including the difficulties faced by women of independent mind.

The most famous poem written by Emma Lazarus (1849–1887) is "The New Colossus," which is inscribed on the pedestal of the Statue of Liberty.

In one of her poems Ella Wheeler Wilcox (1850–1919) wrote, "Laugh, and the world laughs with you; / Weep, and you weep alone."

Among the lovely things of life, poet Sara Teasdale (1884–1933) wrote, were "children's faces looking up / Holding wonder like a cup."

E

In addition to founding a school, Mary McLeod Bethune (1875–1955) created the National Council of Negro Women to advance the cause of African-American women. As a private citizen and as a member of Franklin D. Roosevelt's administration, she worked tirelessly for civil rights. She wrote about education as "the great American adventure" in 1934.

Wrote Emma Willard (1787–1870) in a poem to one of her pupils, "Prosper, and prove a pillar in the cause / Of woman."

"Go forward," Mary Lyon (1797–1849) advised, "attempt great things, accomplish great things."

María Cadilla de Martínez (c. 1886–1951) inspired her students, who in turn inspired others, to study and preserve the traditions and folklore of Puerto Rico.

Anne Sullivan (1866–1936), Helen Keller's teacher, spent her childhood nearly blind. Surgery helped her, but she had difficulties with her vision throughout her life.

Working in the children's division of the New York Public Library, Anne Carroll Moore (1871–1961) revolutionized library practice and helped create a new profession: children's librarian.

F

During several presidencies there was no first lady. James Buchanan was a bachelor. Thomas Jefferson, Andrew Jackson, Martin Van Buren, and Chester Arthur lost their wives before they assumed office. These men often asked female relatives to act as White House hostesses. Two presidents, John Tyler and Woodrow Wilson, lost their wives and remarried while in office.

First ladies are often remembered for special efforts they undertook. Grace Coolidge helped the deaf. Eleanor Roosevelt traveled so that she could tell her husband of people's concerns. Lady Bird Johnson made our country more beautiful by planting flowers, particularly wildflowers. Pat Nixon encouraged volunteerism. Betty Ford inspired candor, particularly about breast cancer. Rosalynn Carter encouraged mental health programs. Nancy Reagan urged young people to "just say no" to drugs. Barbara Bush worked on projects that advance literacy. Hillary Rodham Clinton focused on policies benefiting women and children. Laura Bush encourages all of us, young and old, to read, and she works to foster appreciation of American authors.

Many first ladies have acquired china for the White House, and patterns they selected have inspired the china on the F page. Among the first ladies pictured on patterns they chose are Lucy Hayes, Caroline Harrison, Lady Bird Johnson, Nancy Reagan, and Hillary Rodham Clinton.

G

Frank Leslie's Illustrated Newspaper, a popular nineteenth-century publication, was an inspiration for this page. Although not dedicated to "all the news about women in the news," it was part of a publishing empire headed for many years by a woman, Miriam Folline Leslie, who rescued the company from bankruptcy after the death of her husband, Frank. She legally changed her name to Frank Leslie.

Nellie Bly was the pen name of Elizabeth Cochrane Seaman.

Sui Sin Far's English name was Edith Maude Eaton. Her father was British and her mother Chinese. Almost certainly Sui Sin Far was not an American citizen, but she is included here because she spent most of her adult life in the United States and made an important contribution to American journalism and letters. During the years that Sui Sin Far worked in the United States, Chinese people could not become American citizens because of the Chinese Exclusion Act, which was enacted in 1882 and not repealed until 1943.

H

Eventually Anne and her six youngest children moved to a Dutch colony in New York. There she and five of her children were killed by Indians.

I

Laura Ingalls Wilder published the first of the books about her childhood, *Little House in the Big Woods*, when she was sixty-five. Seven more "Little House" books followed.

The militia that Sybil Ludington helped gather drove the British back to their ships.

Fannie Peck was saving her shoes to wear on the Sabbath, but when Sunday came, she usually couldn't get her shoes on because her feet were sore and swollen.

Ann Maria Weems fled north by means of the Underground Railroad, a system of escape routes established by people opposed to slavery.

J

Anna Jarvis's campaign to establish an official day for mothers resulted in Woodrow Wilson's signing a bill in 1914 designating the second Sunday in May as Mother's Day. Jarvis wanted the day to be about mothers, not presents, and she eventually became disillusioned with the holiday because of what she saw as its commercialization.

Father's Day, first celebrated as a national holiday in 1966, is on the third Sunday in June.

K

Rose Michtom's bear, named in honor of President Teddy Roosevelt, was such a hit that Rose started making lots of teddy bears. One of the first is on exhibit at the Smithsonian Institution today.

L

Pioneer Catherine Sager (1835–1910) lost her birth parents and the parents who subsequently adopted her when she traveled west as a child. She believed that her journey, difficult though it was, would ease the way for those who came after her.

M

Maria Mitchell's observation about women's abilities is quoted in *Maria Mitchell: Life, Letters, and Journals,* a book published by her sister in 1896.

N

Louise Nevelson (c. 1899–1988) assembled pieces of wood into intricate sculptures that were often painted black.

Maria Montoya Martinez (c. 1885–1980) was a ceramic artist who worked with her husband, Julian, to create distinctive black-on-black pottery.

A popular nineteenth-century sculptor, Harriet Hosmer (1830–1908) worked in a velvet beret to keep the marble dust out of her hair.

To create her large abstract paintings, Helen Frankenthaler (1928–   ) sometimes poured thinned pigment onto canvases laid on the floor.

Georgia O'Keeffe (1887–1986) began creating her large flower paintings in the 1920s.

Sarah Peale (1800–1885) was one of America's first successful professional woman artists. Two of her sisters were also painters.

Mary Cassatt (1844–1926) achieved fame as an Impressionist. She often painted women and children.

In the 1960s and 1970s Alma Thomas (1891–1978), who was the first graduate of Howard University's art department, created the bright, densely patterned paintings for which she is most famous.

Author and lecturer Charlotte Perkins Gilman (1860–1935) often took woman's role in society as her subject.

O

Sandra Day O'Connor was appointed to the U.S. Supreme Court in 1981.

Nellie Tayloe Ross became governor of Wyoming in 1925.

Frances Perkins was appointed secretary of labor in 1933.

Jeannette Rankin was elected to the U.S. House of Representatives in 1916.

Esther Morris became justice of the peace in South Pass City, Wyoming, in 1870.

Wilma Mankiller was elected principal chief of the Cherokee Nation in 1987.

P

The curtain on this page was inspired by one in New York City's famed Hippodrome, the spectacular theater that opened in 1905 and was torn down in 1939.

Carol Burnett (1933–) established a comedic landmark with *The Carol Burnett Show*, which ran for eleven years. She ended each show by tugging on her earlobe as a greeting to her grandmother.

Mary Tyler Moore (1936–) won five Emmy Awards for her roles as homemaker Laura Petrie in *The Dick Van Dyke Show* and career girl Mary Richards in *The Mary Tyler Moore Show*.

On *Saturday Night Live*, Gilda Radner (1946–1989) created such unforgettable characters as Roseanne Roseannadanna.

For decades, actress and comedienne Imogene Coca (1908–2001) entertained stage, film, and television audiences with her parodies and lampoons.

Lucille Ball (1911–1989) had the number-one show, *I Love Lucy*, for four television seasons in the 1950s. During the show's peak, two-thirds of American homes with television sets were tuned into it.

Comedienne Fanny Brice (1891–1951) was a *Ziegfeld Follies* star in the 1920s and 1930s. In the 1940s she played Baby Snooks, a bright but bratty child, on radio.

Judith Jamison (1943–) was a principal dancer with the Alvin Ailey American Dance Theater and became the company's artistic director in 1989. *Cry* was her signature dance.

Maria Tallchief (1925–), shown here as the Firebird in George Balanchine's ballet of that name, was prima ballerina with the New York City Ballet and founder and artistic director of the Chicago City Ballet.

Martha Graham (1894–1991) transformed the art of dance with her performances and choreography. One dance she created was *Deep Song*.

At age fifteen Suzanne Farrell (1945–) became the youngest dancer in the history of the New York City Ballet. One of her starring roles was as the Sugar Plum Fairy in *The Nutcracker*.

Isadora Duncan (1878–1927) was a pioneer of modern dance.

Broadway star Mary Martin (1913–1990) is particularly remembered for her starring roles in *South Pacific* and *Peter Pan*.

After dancing more than fifty leading roles with the American Ballet Theater, Lupe Serrano (1930–) became one of America's most honored ballet instructors. One of her memorable roles was in a ballet called *Le Combat*.

Actress and dancer Rita Moreno (1931–) won an Academy Award for her role as Anita in the movie *West Side Story*.

An actress on stage and in film, Ethel Barrymore (1879–1959) became a star in 1901 when she appeared in a play called *Captain Jinks of the Horse Marines*.

Sometimes called the "First Lady of the American Theater," Helen Hayes (1900–1993) was also a success in film, radio, and television. Here she is shown as Queen Victoria in the play *Victoria Regina*.

A musical comedy star of great energy, Ethel Merman (1908–1984) performed in many plays, including *Annie Get Your Gun*.

Actress, singer, and dancer Chita Rivera (1933–) appeared as Anita in the Broadway play *West Side Story* and as Velma Kelly in *Chicago*.

A recording celebrity and a radio and television star, Kate Smith (1907–1986) is most famous for singing "God Bless America."

A singer, actress, and dancer, Lena Horne (1917–) has entertained audiences for more than sixty years. In 1957 she starred in the musical *Jamaica*.

Pearl Bailey (1918–1990) was a much-loved entertainer both in this country and around the world. She debuted on Broadway in *St. Louis Woman*.

Angela Lansbury (1925–) received an Oscar nomination in 1944 and over the next six decades continued her successful acting career. *Murder, She Wrote*, a television series in which she starred, was the highest-rated television drama for nine straight seasons.

A child star with a powerful voice, Judy Garland (1922–1969) starred as Dorothy in *The Wizard of Oz*. As an adult she made dozens of movies and performed in concert.

A jazz singer, Ella Fitzgerald (1917–1996) won thirteen Grammy Awards during her fifty-year career.

Aretha Franklin (1942–) began singing gospel music when she was a girl and went on to become one of the greatest recording stars of all time. In 1987 she was the first woman inducted into the Rock and Roll Hall of Fame.

Tina Turner (1939–) was inducted into the Rock and Roll Hall of Fame in 1991. She was the top touring act of the year 2000.

Leontyne Price (1927–) toured in a revival of *Porgy and Bess*, sang the lead in a television production of *Tosca*, and appeared as Cleopatra in *Antony and Cleopatra* at the opening of the new Metropolitan Opera House in 1966.

Carol Channing (1921–) became a legend as Dolly in the musical *Hello, Dolly!*

Contralto Marian Anderson (1897–1993) began singing in church when she was six years old and as an adult frequently included spirituals in her programs. When she was not allowed to appear in Constitution Hall because she was African American, an outdoor concert was held at the Lincoln Memorial and 75,000 people came to hear her sing.

A coloratura soprano, Beverly Sills (1929–) has won accolades for her success as a performer and for her work as general director of the New York City Opera and chairman of the Lincoln Center for the Performing Arts.

Among those who loved to hear famed gospel singer Mahalia Jackson (1911–1972) sing "Precious Lord Take My Hand" was Dr. Martin Luther King Jr. In 1968 Jackson sang the song at Dr. King's funeral.

Patsy Cline (1932–1963), who died when she was just thirty, is an American music legend. In 1973 she was elected to the Country Music Hall of Fame.

A gifted pianist, Hazel Harrison (1883–1969) spent her life perfecting her talent. Because of racial segregation, she could not perform in America's major concert halls, but she built an enormous following nonetheless.

A mezzo-soprano, Marilyn Horne (1934–) has performed in the great opera houses of the world. She began singing at the piano before she was two years old.

Grace Kelly (1929–1982) starred in such film classics as *High Noon* and *Rear Window* before marrying Prince Rainier of Monaco and retiring from filmmaking.

As a girl Camilla Urso (1842–1902) begged to play the violin, which many people at the time thought was an instrument only for boys. She grew up to become one of the outstanding violinists of her era.

Actress Rita Hayworth (1918–1987), who epitomized Hollywood glamour during the 1940s, started her career as a dancer.

Sophie Tucker (1884–1966), who immigrated to the United States from Russia as a small child, used her booming voice to become a popular vaudeville entertainer.

Marilyn Monroe (1926–1962), known for her glamour, also had a flare for comedy.

As a four-year-old Shirley Temple (1928–) showed remarkable talent for dancing, singing, and acting, and she became Hollywood's biggest box-office attraction. As an adult she became U.S. ambassador to Ghana and Czechoslovakia.

After a successful career as a movie star, Lauren Bacall (1924–) moved to the stage and won Tony Awards for her roles in *Applause* and *Woman of the Year*.

Ginger Rogers (1911–1995) made ten memorable musicals with her dance partner Fred Astaire. She also won an Oscar for best actress in 1940.

Urged by her father to study ballet, Cyd Charisse (1921–) grew up to star in classic films like *The Band Wagon* and *Brigadoon*.

The most famous movie role played by Rosalind Russell (1907–1976) was the title role in *Auntie Mame*. Her most famous line in that movie was "Life is a banquet."

Film star Barbara Stanwyck (1907–1990) appeared in mysteries, comedies, and westerns.

Joan Crawford (1904–1977) began her career as a dancer, did musical films, and then drama. She won an Oscar in 1945.

Myrna Loy (1905–1993) first became famous playing Nora Charles in the Thin Man series of films.

After great success as a silent film star, Gloria Swanson (1897–1983) retired from the screen after sound films arrived. She made a memorable comeback in 1950 in the movie *Sunset Boulevard*.

Katharine Hepburn (1907–) has played strong, independent women on stage and screen. As a film actress she won a record four Academy Awards.

A star for nearly six decades, actress Bette Davis (1908–1989) appeared in more than one hundred films. She is shown here as she appeared in *The Private Lives of Elizabeth and Essex*.

For her performances, actress Jessica Tandy (1909–1994) won Tony Awards, an Oscar, and an Emmy. In 1994 she received a lifetime achievement award for her accomplishments on Broadway.

Judy Holliday (1921–1965) is often remembered for her role as Billie Dawn in *Born Yesterday,* a play that became a film and earned her an Oscar.

An actress of remarkable resilience, Academy Award–winning Patricia Neal (1926–) has been a star in plays and on film. Her Oscar was for her 1963 performance in *Hud*.

Although Cincinnati was her birthplace, Theda Bara (1885–1955) pretended to have been born "in the shadow of the Sphinx." The exotic role she assumed made her a star of silent films.

Conductor Sarah Caldwell (1924–) gave violin recitals before she was ten and graduated from high school at age fourteen. In 1957 she founded the Opera Company of Boston.

R

Although Women Airforce Service Pilots (WASP) flew almost every kind of aircraft in World War II and thirty-eight of them lost their lives doing so, they were considered civilians. Not until 1979 were they granted military status.

The illustration of the women who autographed the plane is based on a 1943 photograph in the picture collection of the New York Public Library.

S

Susan B. Anthony's great-niece and namesake is second from left in the illustration. Among those with her are tennis champion Billie Jean King, Congresswoman Bella Abzug, and Betty Friedan, who wrote *The Feminine Mystique*.

The photograph that inspired this illustration shows the finish of a 1977 marathon meant to call attention to the Equal Rights Amendment (ERA), which was passed by the U.S. Congress in 1972 but failed to be ratified by a sufficient number of states. The women in the picture believed the ERA was important to women's progress, but other women disagreed and campaigned against it.

T

The author of *Woman as Force in History*, Mary Beard (1876–1958) set the stage for scholars who would come after her to write about women's contributions.

For her efforts to improve health-care services, Annie Dodge Wauneka (1910–1997) was awarded the Presidential Medal of Freedom.

Marjory Stoneman Douglas (1890–1998) wrote *The Everglades: River of Grass*, which called attention to an environmental treasure.

Antoinette Blackwell (1825–1921) was ordained as a Congregational Church minister in 1853.

Joan Ganz Cooney (1929–) spearheaded the creation of Children's Television Workshop and *Sesame Street*.

Peggy Charren (1928–) founded Action for Children's Television to reform children's television.

Elizabeth Peabody (1804–1894) opened the first U.S. kindergarten in 1860.

Charlotte Ray (1850–1911) graduated from Howard University School of Law in 1872 and was admitted to the District of Columbia bar shortly thereafter.

When Amelia Bloomer (1818–1894) defended women wearing the skirt-and-pantaloon combination, the outfit was quickly dubbed the "Bloomer costume," or "bloomers."

Julia Morgan (1872–1957) is best known for designing William Randolph Hearst's castle at San Simeon, California.

In 1905 Muriel Strode (1875–1946) wrote about blazing a trail in *My Little Book of Prayer*.

U

In a two-page history many notable events and achievements must go unacknowledged, and children should be encouraged to add to this time line. The Statue of Liberty at the top of the page, for example, might be an opportunity to talk about Emma Lazarus's poem "The New Colossus," which is inscribed on the statue's pedestal. Children can also place in the time line figures from other pages in this book. Where does Abigail Adams fit? Emily Dickinson? Mary McLeod Bethune?

W

Edith Wharton (1862–1937) won the Pulitzer Prize for her novel *The Age of Innocence*.

Pearl S. Buck (1892–1973), who grew up in China, became the first American woman to win the Nobel Prize for literature.

Legend has it that when Abraham Lincoln met Harriet Beecher Stowe (1811–1896) after the Civil War had started, he said, "So this is the little lady who wrote the book that made this great war."

Encouraged by her mother to aspire mightily, Zora Neale Hurston (c. 1901–1960) became an author. Her best-known work is the novel *Their Eyes Were Watching God*.

Influenced by her physician-father, Sarah Orne Jewett (1849–1909) grew up to love and write about the New England region in which she was born. *The Country of the Pointed Firs* is her best-known work.

With novels like *Sula* and *Beloved* that explore African-American experience, Toni Morrison (1931–) has become one of America's most noted writers. In 1993 she won the Nobel Prize.

Louisa May Alcott (1832–1888) wrote *Little Women,* a novel beloved by generations of American girls.

Willa Cather (1873–1947) won the Pulitzer Prize for her 1922 novel, *One of Ours.*

In her book *Borderlands,* Gloria Anzaldúa (1942–) writes about growing up between two cultures, Mexican and Anglo.

The best-known work of Carson McCullers (1917–1967) is *The Member of the Wedding,* a novel that became a play.

For her novel *The Color Purple,* Alice Walker (1944–) won the Pulitzer Prize. She has also edited an anthology of the work of Zora Neale Hurston.

Mary O'Hara (1885–1980) wrote *My Friend Flicka,* a book about a boy and a horse that became a movie and a television series. Another of her books, *Green Grass of Wyoming,* also became a movie.

Ayn Rand (1905–1982) said that the theme of her life was "individualism." That was also the theme of her novels *The Fountainhead* and *Atlas Shrugged.*

Encouraged by her grandmother, Katherine Anne Porter (c. 1890–1980) grew up to write short fiction and a novel, *Ship of Fools.* In 1966 she won the Pulitzer Prize.

Mary McCarthy (1912–1989) often wrote satire, a form of writing that aims to show how foolish people can be. Her best-known work is a novel, *The Group.*

Margaret Wise Brown (1910–1952) wrote more than one hundred books for children, including *Goodnight Moon.*

Although Kate Chopin (c. 1851–1904) did not begin her career as an author until she was in her late thirties, she published many short stories and a novel that is held in high regard today: *The Awakening.*

Mari Sandoz (1896–1966) wrote stories about people who inhabited the Great Plains of the United States. *Old Jules, Crazy Horse,* and *The Buffalo Hunters* are among her books.

In her most famous story, "Seventeen Syllables," Hisaye Yamamoto (1921–) considered what immigration to the United States meant to the first generation of Japanese Americans and their children.

Ellen Glasgow (1873–1945), who spent most of her life in Richmond, Virginia, often took as her theme the emergence of a "New South." She won the Pulitzer Prize in 1942.

Edna Ferber (1885–1968) began her writing career as a reporter and went on to author many novels featuring strong women. Her book *Giant* was made into a famous movie.

Flannery O'Connor (1925–1964), who raised peacocks on her farm, wrote short stories and novels that were often funny and serious at the same time.

In her work Annie Dillard (1945–) pays close attention to nature. She won the Pulitzer Prize for *Pilgrim at Tinker Creek.*

The diary that Mary Chesnut (1823–1886) kept portrays Southern life and personalities during the Civil War.

Mary Antin (1881–1949), who came to the United States from Russia when she was thirteen, wrote about the opportunities America offers in *The Promised Land.*

Margaret Mitchell (1900–1949) wrote *Gone with the Wind,* an epic novel of the South and the Civil War that became the best-selling novel in history.

Edith Hamilton (1867–1963), who learned Greek and Latin as a child, grew up to write *The Greek Way* and *The Roman Way,* books that conveyed her sense of the noble ideals of antiquity.

Mary Mapes Dodge (1831–1905), whose first published stories were ones she had told to her sons, wrote the classic book *Hans Brinker: or, The Silver Skates.* She was also editor of the children's magazine *St. Nicholas.*

A key question writers should ask, said Catherine Drinker Bowen (1897–1973), the author of widely read biographies, is, "Will the reader turn the page?"

Zitkala Ša (1876–1938) was the tribal name of Gertrude Bonnin, an author who drew on her Yankton Sioux heritage in her writing. She was the author of *Old Indian Legends* and *American Indian Stories.*

Marjorie Kinnan Rawlings (1896–1953) wrote *The Yearling,* a novel about a boy who adopts a fawn as his pet. *The Yearling* won the Pulitzer Prize and was made into a movie.

Shirley Jackson (1916–1965) could write funny stories, such as those she wrote about raising children, but her best-known work, "The Lottery," makes readers think rather than laugh.

In her novel *To Kill a Mockingbird,* Harper Lee (1926–) depicts a girl named Scout Finch coming to understand how wrong prejudice is.

An award-winning writer of history, Esther Forbes (1891–1967) wrote a historical novel for young people that has become a classic: *Johnny Tremain.*

Labor activist and author Tillie Olsen (1913–) observed how hard it was for most women, given their many responsibilities, to find time to write.

Margaret Bayard Smith (1778–1844), who moved to Washington, D.C., when it first became the nation's capital, wrote letters and kept notes describing her experiences that were published as *The First Forty Years of Washington Society.*

X
In this illustration Sojourner Truth, Lucretia Mott, Martha Coffin Wright, and Lucy Stone stand for all those, in addition to Anthony and Stanton, who worked for suffrage but did not live to see American women's right to vote fully recognized.

Y
Women achievers in science have had to overcome especially strong stereotypes. When Rosalyn Yalow received an A– in a lab class, she was told it was evidence that women were unsuited for laboratory work. Gertrude Elion had trouble finding a job in a laboratory until World War II called men into service. Maria Goeppert Mayer, married to a chemist, was often without a full-time job because of university rules that prohibited employment of both husband and wife.

Z
Helen Reddy won a Grammy Award in 1973 for her performance of "I Am Woman."